Getting Your Music Heard Online

a collection of articles written by

Joshua Smotherman

and

C Bret Campbell

for

Middle Tennessee Music.com

This book includes articles written and published by Joshua Smotherman and C Bret Campbell to their website, MiddleTennesseeMusic.com.

This information focuses on using the Internet and Social Media to promote and market music as a do-it-yourself musician, songwriter, artist, band, or other entity involved in the music business.
As we continue using the web to promote our own music and help others promote theirs, we will update this book on a regular basis with new articles and information.

As someone who purchased and downloaded this book, you will receive these updates for free.

The free updates are our way of saying thank You for your support and interest in our mission to continue the discussion about the Internet and music as a business with indie musicians worldwide.

Contact Joshua: joshua@midtnmusic.com
Contact Bret: bret@midtnmusic.com

Middle Tennessee Music came into being as a website in May of 2011. Our mission is to empower independent musicians online. We accomplish this by featuring album reviews, event promotion, and interviews. We also publish informational articles sharing our research and experiences with marketing music online.

We also share the resources, tools, books, and strategies we have used over the years to get our music heard across the planet using the interwebs.

This book was written by indie musicians for indie musicians.
www.MiddleTennesseeMusic.com

Table of Contents

Bonus *(not published on MTM)*

How To Get Your Music Heard

The world is changing, especially the music world. It seems every day there is another act on the verge. Every time you log onto the net (does anyone log off anymore?) there is another company telling you why they are the best thing since electricity for promoting your music, and another website clamoring for your membership. Well...

Don't Believe the Hype - Create It!

A few things are, for the moment, certain.

- An unknown band can become a sensation.
- Becoming a sensation today won't keep you from being old hat tomorrow.
- You have to work to succeed.

Where do you start?

The very first step (assuming you have mastered the art of making great music) is to make great music. Sounds redundant, but it's not. Is your music something the public will want to listen to? If not, they won't listen to it. Find a way to make even the weirdest of noise sound fun and familiar.

Play at least one live show every week, even if that means your are set up in the park with nothing but an acoustic guitar, and hoping "the man" doesn't come to run you off.

Build a website! Having your own domain name shows you are serious. It gives you a place to consolidate all the important aspects of your career. It is also your fall-back position for when things go sour with your free pages elsewhere.

Spread the word

Assuming you have polished your act, made some high quality

recordings, and built an enjoyable website:

You need to utilize social media but maintaining 100 profiles on different sites is ridiculous. Figure out which ones will give you the most bang for your buck and put all your energy there.

Using videos and YouTube is highly recommended.

You will use these pages to meet and communicate with fans, venues, industry professionals, etcetera. This will be how the public gets to know you and your music. Most importantly, this is where the public will form their opinion of you and your brand.

Once you have begun to build a little bit of a following, you will want to take further steps to

Assure Easy Access to your Music.

- Make certain that your songs are on your band pages, link your Reverb page or your Bandcamp page to your website.
- Offer at least one, preferably a few songs, for free download. You might want to offer an unfinished studio cut of one of your more popular songs. This allows the listener to feel like he is part of the creation process.
- It will take some doing, and you will need a good following, but get your music on Spotify, Pandora, and any other streaming service you can.

Build the Buzz

- When trying to get noticed by a record label, you need something to show that you are somebody. It is advised by Berkley and other professional schools and organizations that you be able to present no less than 200 articles, write ups, blog mentions, or other publications that feature your act.

- Even if you only offer audio with scrolling lyrics on YouTube, you want to utilize it, as you may be able to say that, currently, it is "America's jukebox". You need video so that it can be embedded into the articles and posts written about and by you.

- You should submit to as many on-line independent radio stations as you can. These stations are a Fantastic way to build a buzz, and many do live interviews and co-hosting with their artists, such as @AllIndie on #TwitterTuesdayLive.

Think Global! Your home-town is by necessity where you will begin, but your friends can only support you to a certain degree. Practice your show for them, and learn from their reaction to your music, then spread it out. As you dig into social media and develop a tight group of professional friends around the globe, you'll be amazed at what can be accomplished.

How To Get Featured On More Music Blogs

This article is not a how-to in the sense I will give you step-by-step instructions to getting your music featured on more blogs...

Instead, my goal is to take your thinking to a higher level in order to understand some bigger concepts that will enhance your overall promotion strategies.

When I'm not wrangling toddlers or taking a puppy out to potty, I spend my time acting as a music blogger and a music promoter; but I am also a songwriter and producer.

I walk both sides of this blogging / submission line.

When I write about these things I'm speaking from experience more than anything else.

Let's get into it.

Attitude

On the Internet, your attitude means everything.

If you are a negative person, an introvert, or expect everyone to rush to you and start treating you like a rock star because you think you are awesome; then don't waste your time using the Internet to promote music.

The thing you need to understand is you are in the game of relationship marketing.

This means connecting with everyday people like you, like me, and like your favorite blogger you read everyday.

Whether you think so or not, your attitude comes across in your emails. It shows up on your website, your EPK, and everywhere else you are putting yourself online.

If you are giving bloggers a bad taste upon first impression, you will not be featured.

However, showing a little respect and being nice can go a long way.

For example:

In the event you are not sure how to be featured on a blog, sending a one line email asking how to be featured goes a lot further than an email telling the blogger you want to be featured.

This may sound ridiculous but it happens. All. The. Time.

Attention to small details goes a long way.

Tell a story

This one is simple.

One thing that separates a good submission from a bad submission is when there is a story behind the music.

80% of the time when a band submits materials to us they simply send a list of links. If we are lucky, we receive a short bio or description of the music.

Why do you think VH1's Behind the Music was such a popular series?

The harder a blogger has to work to get into your music, the further your chances of being featured decrease.

When we receive submissions from PR firms or independent promoters, who represent artists and songwriters as their clients, we receive a very polished bio with a bit of band history as well as a list of accolades and awards (if they exist).

These submissions are always accompanied by great photos, mp3s, and links to everything a blogger would want to know about a band. They also, conveniently, include a list of popular bands that are similar in style so we know what to expect before clicking play.

Including these comparisons also helps blogs determine which writer best connects with a submission (if multiple authors exist).

It is safe to assume more of these submissions get featured.

But the good news is you do not need a PR firm to put together a great submission package.

Strategy

This is probably as important as your attitude.

If you have no goal or have no clue what you are doing, you will fail.

The beautiful thing about this is you are in control. You get to make these decisions. No waiting for permission or approvals to move forward.

Whether you spend 30 minutes a day or 40 hours a week, you need to have some sort of outline with reasonable goals to achieve.

When you are trying to find blogs to feature your music, you can spend as much as 4 hours a day or as little as 10 minutes a day searching Google for music blogs in your genre. It doesn't matter but **be consistent.**

The next step is to find blogs that you think are **relevant** to your style of music.
You need to look through the previous articles posted on these blogs, get a sense of what the authors like in music, and then decide if they would write favorably about yours.

If you can locate 3 to 5 blogs a day, you have made a list of 21 to 35 potential features in 1 week. If you can get featured on half of those, you have created a decent buzz. As long as you don't stop or give up, the buzz will keep buzzing.

As you do this you want to make a list, taking note of the blogs website address, the author (or authors) who you think like your music, how to contact them, and make sure you **follow the**

directions the blog gives for submitting music (if directions are provided).

I highly recommend **creating a spreadsheet**. This will help you organize your blog contacts and keep them for future reference.

If you do not have Microsoft Excel, you can use Google Drive's spreadsheet feature free of charge.

One important thing to remember about your strategy is to not blindly submit to blogs.

Do. Your. Research.

This does not mean spend countless hours over-thinking the process but simply show a little common courtesy by getting to know the blog and bloggers before sending your music for consideration.

If you can geniunely come across as a reader of the blog, it will spark attention and raise your chances of being noticed. It is ok to say things like, "I enjoyed your review of XYZ band, our music is similar but with ABC twist" in your submission e-mail.

You need to say more than that, but you get the idea.

Conclusion

These 3 concepts can tremendously help you up your blog marketing game. Just remember 1) you are not a rock star and 2) you are connecting with people. If you can do this you will be fine.

Do not underestimate the power of the follow-up. If a few weeks have gone by and you have not heard back from a blog you submitted to, send a quick follow up and ask if they received your original submission.

Sometimes e-mails are unintentionally missed or sometimes even opened with the intention of remembering to get back to you but distractions often cause people to be forgetful.

You should also assume bloggers receive a lot more e-mails per day than the average person. Be patient and be respectful.

Why Your Music Is Not Getting Heard

Over the past year and a half, we have been fortunate enough to reach a point where we are overwhelmed with independent music to listen to and write about.

With this abundance of tunes, we now have to pick and choose the *crème de la crème*. It also means we have the unfortunate task of rejecting EPKs and other submissions received from awesome people like you.

Many times an artist or band sounds great but they just don't have their presentation together. This will cause them to be ignored.

You must realize that thousands of bands are fighting for attention in this space. ***Stand out***.

You have to grab the attention of the blogger, radio DJ, music editor, or whoever you are targeting...and grab it hard.

Here is my #1 reason for rejecting submissions.

Your EPK (or Presentation) Sucks

Allow me to break this down.

1. Bio (or about info)

One of the first things I do when receiving a new music submission is read the bio.

This is a good indicator of what level you are at in your career and how serious you are about music as a career. You can immediately tell the difference between a hobbyist and someone surviving gig to gig.

It's also obvious when a PR person writes it or you have done your own research and learned to write an "industry-style" bio.

If your bio says, "we smoke a lot of pot".... yeah, I'm not featuring you. And, yes, this happened recently.

I don't know why, but rappers have a **<u>horrible</u>** habit of typing in all caps.

I ignored an artist earlier because their BIO WAS ALL CAPS...it was a few paragraphs long, too. The cat had an inspiring story and he had a high quality video; but you should know better than to yell at people.

2. Photos

Your photos are typically the first thing we see when introduced to your band. This means you have to make a great first impression.

Photos can be the difference between clicking play or skipping to the next submission.

It is inevitable you will need to invest in a photographer (or find a friend/intern) that knows how to use a camera.

3. Video

These days everyone and their mama has a camera capable of HD so producing a great video isn't necessarily that hard of a task to accomplish.

Again, the key is to **stand out**, be unique, and tell a story (or make a statement).

Just because you filmed yourself jamming out in the garage with an HD camera doesn't necessarily mean you have an awesome video. It's highly likely other bands have done this time and time again so you need to do something to make yours stand above the others.

If your video is poor quality (or has great picture with horrible sound), you will be skipped.

4. Links

This should be a no brainer, but bands that have their own websites stand far above the ones that only have a Facebook page.

Having www.yourband.com as a link in your submission shows people how serious you take yourself. It also proves that you are investing time and money into your music which indicates a certain level of dedication and drive.

If you include no links, you will definitely be ignored.

Personally, I like being able to visit your website and a social media profile. If I am going to feature you, I want to learn as much as I can before writing.

5. Website - www.yourband.com

Like photos, your website is responsible for making a first impression on people.

Your website is your business card. Treat it that way.

A 1) visually appealing, 2) well organized, 3) easy to navigate website will receive way more attention than a cluttered, ugly one.

Also, the more info you include about yourself and your music, the better. If I have to dig longer than 2 minutes to find your bio or any information about your band, I skip you and move on to the next submission.

When we build websites for bands, we recommend a minimum number of pages including: Bio, Music, Photos, and Contact.

We also highly recommend blogging for many reasons, but that's for a future article.

Depending on how much you have going on, you might need additional pages such as: Shows, Press, Videos, or Store.

Bonus Tip (my process)

When one is overwhelmed with submissions (like most media outlets), one will naturally develop a system for filtering out the bad ones.

I will share my (current) quick n' dirty decision process with you.

- **Bio**: If it is well written, tells a great story, or proves to me you are serious about music as a career – I definitely click play and I typically end up on your website or connect with you on social networks. Mentioning awards, accolades, and recognition definitely grabs my attention.
- **Photos**: If you include none or unappealing ones, it is a turn off and causes me to 2nd guess whether or not to click play.

- **Video**: If you submit one, I almost always click play. If I like it, then I will listen to more of your music and visit your website.
- **Music**: I typically decide within the first 30 seconds if I am going to continue listening to a song or skip to the next. With that said, unless you have an interesting story behind your song – those first 30 seconds better make me want to keep listening.
- **Links:** If you link to www.yourband.com, you receive more attention than someone who only links to a Facebook page or ReverbNation profile. It shows a level of commitment to your career and proves that you are investing money and time into presenting yourself properly. (*Make sure your site looks great.*)

Are you struggling to get more exposure for your music?

4 Simple Steps To Improve Your Chances At Being Promoted On Music Blogs

We'll keep this one short and simple.

If you're like me, you've got diapers to change, mouths to feed, work to do, and no time to do any of it.

Such is life.

So you want or maybe need to know how to get your music promoted through the Blogosphere?

Here's some advice that will improve your chances.

Do some research

I know, I know. It takes a little bit of time and that "research" word scares people, but take a deep breath and slap yourself in the face.

To avoid appearing ignorant to the bloggers, that you want to build relationships with, dig around their blogs a little before submitting material.

Don't forget to leave comments on some of the posts. Us bloggers pay closer attention to people who leave comments on our site.

Take note of what artists have already been featured and what the writers on the site have had to say about the bands and their songs.

Follow their directions...please

Most bloggers that openly accept submissions will have a page or button that will take you to directions or instructions on how to submit your material.

Make sure you follow them.

If you only find an e-mail address, then there are 4 items you should include in your e-mail to make the blogger's life easier (and yes we love it when you do).

1. Short Bio (1 page or less) or some type of description or background info about your song
2. Photo(s) and/or a link to your EPK or video
3. Attach an MP3 or include a link where one can be listened to
4. Include links to your Official Website and/or Twitter, Facebook, YouTube, ReverbNation and other social media sites

Try not to sound like an idiot in your submission e-mail

TYPING IN ALL CAPS IS LIKE YELLING IN MY FACE.

DON'T DO IT!

And try using spell check.

Also try those things known as grammar and punctuation.

You need to say more than *"check out my music"*

It's really irritating when we get an e-mail that says.

go check out my music. http://www.whyshoudi.com

Seriously? Not even a hello?

Most bloggers are blogging to build or improve their network.

We enjoy interacting with people and we like to build relationships.

You should be trying to build relationships with the bloggers you submit to.

This one simple act can improve the likelihood of having your music promoted in the future.

Top 3 Ways To Submit Music to Bloggers and Press

You have your album finished. You have a couple of music videos ready to support the strongest singles. And you have taken time to find a list of blogs you think might feature your music.

What is the best way to submit your music to bloggers and press?

The following are simply my recommendations based on years of experience accepting music submissions from bands.

As a blogger, there is nothing I hate more than having to spend 10 minutes digging up your bio, finding a song to stream, or locating your YouTube or Facebook link on your website.

As long as you:

- Follow each blog's submissions guidelines,
- Have all your information and music easily accessible,

- And have music worth listening to...

Then you should be just fine.

My other tip is to **make sure you are targeting relevant blogs** (and press outlets) that have previously featured music in the same sphere as yours. Sending dope boy gangsta rap to an alternative hip hop blog will NOT get you featured.

Here are my top 3 music submission methods.

Soundcloud or Bandcamp

I like to click a link and then click play.

Soundcloud and Bandcamp allow me to do both...quickly and efficiently.
I also prefer these two platforms because I can easily copy and paste an embed code into a blog post.

ReverbNation works as well but I find myself liking this method (maybe even the platform) less and less.

The only down-side is not having instant access to a bio or more info about the band.

Unfortunately, most bands are horrible at maintaining good profiles. They need to read Bret's series on creating attractive ones.

EPK Services

If you are using a service such as MusicSUBMIT, Sonicbids, Onesheet, or ReverbNation's RPK to share your music, bio, photos, and links with the press and bloggers, then you are one step ahead of everybody else.

Why do I like this one? Simple.

*I can click a link and **all the information (I want) is right there**.*

If you are using a paid service (Sonicbids, ReverbNation), it also shows us that you are investing money into marketing. This makes you stand out because it shows a more serious commitment to the music and developing it into a career (it does not necessarily mean you make good music though).

Dropbox

I am also a fan of just downloading a good ole fashioned .zip file...as long as it contains everything a proper EPK should.

I have been using **Dropbox** *(referral link)* for file sharing and cloud storage for a couple of years at this point...and I love it.

Now that they have updated their share links feature, it is easier to share files with anyone.

There are other large file sending and sharing sites such as YouSendIt or Mediafire, but Dropbox is the one that has won my heart.

Earlier this morning a band used Dropbox to send me a .zip file of their EPK. I quickly e-mailed them back and said thank you for making it easy for me to get all the information... This does not happen every day.

If you use this method, your .zip file should include:

- album (I prefer mp3s because 1) small file sizes, 2) quick downloads, 3) bandwidth saved.)
- album cover (most bands forget this one)
- bio
- photos (5 maximum – just my opinion)
- a document or one sheet containing your links and/or any additional information (press releases, awards, tour schedule)

Derek Sivers (creator/founder of CD Baby) published an article with one of the best tips I have heard yet: a promo box on your desktop.

A lot of times less is more...but in this case I prefer receiving more than I need to avoid digging it up myself. (I thoroughly research bands before I write about them so if all their info is in one place...)

When you make a blogger or journalist's life easier, you make them happy. This leads to features and new fans.

Bonus Tips

Do NOT blindly list the first 100 blogs you find that feature music in your genre. This is not effective and will be a waste.

You need to take your time, set reasonable goals, and do your research.

Try finding 5 to 10 blogs each day (if you have the time). Look through the articles that have already been published and develop a strategy before sending your first e-mail.
If you personalize each e-mail to each blogger, you will significantly increase your chances of being noticed.

The only way to do this is to learn by digging through their recent posts. If there are multiple bloggers, find one that features music like yours. Sending death metal to the guy that writes about power pop will get you ignored.

Find a band or artist similar to you that was previously featured and mention them in your submission e-mail. It not only alerts the blogger to your sound but also lets them know you have been paying attention to their site.

If you really want to put yourself on a blogger's radar, visit the site regularly and comment on new posts as they are published. Getting involved in blog communities increases your chances at being noticed even more. It also puts you on the radar of everyone else in the community.

Typically blogs keep a blogroll in their sidebar. A blogroll is a list of links to other blogs. Once you find one or two you want to submit to, you should be able to use their blogrolls to continue finding more (relevant) blogs.

I suggest avoiding blog directories (except as a last resort).

The alternative to the do-it-yourself approach is to hire a PR firm.

What Are ID3 Tags and How To Edit Them

You know what is annoying? And you know what probably annoys radio personnel more than it annoys me?

Lack of ID3 tags when you submit your music.

Even worse than lacking ID3 tags is when a band doesn't even take the time to name their files properly...but that is for another discussion.

If you are sending your music to bloggers, press, podcasters, radio, or putting it anywhere on the Internet, **make sure your MP3s are labeled properly and you have included ID3 tags.**

What happens if you fail to accomplish this task?

Your songs look like this when we load them into our media players:

1. Unknown – Track 01

2. Unknown – Track 02

3. Unknown – Track 03

We (bloggers, etc) have no clue what band we are hearing.

Epic promotion failure.

Sidebar: When I worked for an independent publisher, one of my most important jobs was checking and editing file names and ID3 tags before any song left the office. That's how important this is.

What are ID3 tags?

The process of including data in an audio file is known as *tagging*.

ID3 tags are, basically, a data container attached to an audio file. ID3 is specific to MP3 and MP3 Pro formats.

WAV files have no tags. WMA, OGG, and AAC all use different standards for tagging (not ID3).

This standard was developed in 1996 by Eric Kemp. ID3 simply means "IDtentify an MP3".

ID3 tags allow you to include the Album Title, Track Title, Artist/Band Name, Copyright Info, as well as several other bits of information. You are also able to include a thumbnail image (which is how you make your album cover show up in Windows Media Player, etc).

Instead of boring you with all the technical details, you can read more and learn the history by visiting ID3.org.

How do I edit ID3 tags?

This is not as hard as you might think.

I prefer a program called Mp3tag, but there are plenty of options available.

If you use iTunes, you can edit your tags with that.

Lifehacker published the Six Best MP3 Tagging Tools so I will let them alert you to the other options.

Now take this knowledge and (please) apply it!

Resources

- ID3.org
- Download MP3tag
- Six Best MP3 Tagging Tools by Jason Fitzpatrick (on Lifehacker.com)

3 Common Music Marketing Mistakes Artists Make Using Social Media

Jumping right in.

Never thanking or engaging with new and current fans

I have found, from personal experience, that I'm more likely to listen to your music (or visit your website or like you on Facebook) if I receive a "thank you" from an artist or musician after becoming their fan.

It doesn't have to be anything elaborate. The majority of people do not have time to read long messages.

I have also found that when I take a few moments to send thank yous to my new fans and followers, it usually leads to further interaction with those people. I have developed several beneficial relationships simply by taking some time each day to send a note of gratitude.

In other words, treat people like you want to be treated

You never know who might start following you.

Beware of the loonie toonies though. Oddballs exist everywhere.

Stop talking about yourself all the time

Nothing is more boring, and usually annoying, than people who use their status updates to demand everyone go download their new song.

Go look at your Twitter timeline. If 7 out of your last 10 tweets say the same thing or are only promoting yourself, you are NOT using social media to your advantage.
In fact you are doing the opposite.

Ever wonder how many of your 345 followers actually pay attention to your Tweets?
If you are only talking about yourself, chances are not that many.

It's time you start Re-Tweeting interesting or relevant Tweets from your followers, replying and thanking them for @mentioning you, or commenting back on their profile when they take the time to leave you one.

Hell, take a couple of seconds each morning and ask your fans a question and begin conversation(s).

Engage with others and they will engage with you.

Never listening to other people's music and leaving them comments

This one is simple.

If you are not out in the community (online or in deez skreets) paying attention to other artists and musicians, then why would you expect them to pay attention to you.

Developing relationships with other bands, artists, and musicians is an excellent method for exponentially expanding your fan base on a much broader scale than working it solo.

This is called the World Wide Web for a reason.

The best way I know to get people to comment on your music is to go **listen** to their songs and **leave comments**...

Build a community.

And make sure you say more than "nice song". Put a little thought into it and don't hesitate to be critical.

The real artists appreciate honest feedback.

5 Valuable Resources Every Musician Needs To Know About

Below are 5 very valuable resources containing an abundance of information about moving forward with a DIY marketing strategy.

1. The Buzz Factor (Bob Baker)

Bob Baker is the author of books such as:

- Guerilla Music Marketing Handbook
- Guerilla Music Marketing Online
- Unleash the Artist Within
- Killer Music Press Kits
- Killer Music Web Sites
- and many more...

Reading the Guerilla Music Marketing Handbook was probably the most pivotal point in my life.

It's safe to say its his fault we're doing what we do now.

2. Derek Sivers

Derek Sivers is responsible for that little thing known as CD Baby. He sold the company to DiscMakers and now does his own thing.

I highly recommend following his blog and looking through his website. He knows his stuff and well, just go check it out.

Make sure you download his FREE e-book. You won't regret it.

3. Music Think Tank

As their website says, *this is where the music industry thinks out loud.*

My favorite part of MTT is that it is an open forum and anyone can contribute. Below is the first paragraph you see when visiting the site.

Anyone can contribute relevant articles to Music Think Tank. Begin by signing up and then logging in to publish your posts directly to MTT Open; popular articles are occasionally moved to the front of the site. Contributors own and operate this blog (more info). Founded March 4th, 2008. Interested sponsors: please review our stats prior to contacting us.

Another dope aspect of the site is MTT Radio, where anyone can post a song and be heard by their audience. They are visited by approximately 25,000 music industry readers every month. Sweet!!

4. Indie Guide

This site is one big database of resources any musician or band needs to survive independently. They also have really helpful e-books available.

And if you are really serious, these guys publish The Indie Bible and The Indie Venue Bible.

5. Artists House Music

Helping Musicians and Music Entrepreneurs Create Sustainable Careers

A WEALTH of information about everything in the music business. Legal, Production, Marketing Strategies, the list keeps going and you get it all in a variety of formats including videos, articles, and open discussions.

I highly suggest you check it out.

More Helpful Links

- mi2n.com – site that allows you to submit Press Releases for distribution to their network
- Ariel Publicity – Digital PR Firm and an educational experience wrapped up in one
- GenY Rock Stars – home of the New Music Economy
- Kacey Jones Songwriting Workshop – improve your songwriting with one of the best
- Home Studio Corner – learn all you need to know about recording your music

5 Valuable Sites You Might Not Be Using To Promote Your Music

With over 34 million blogs on their servers, Tumblr is a networking goldmine.

Why do I likeTumblr? Simplicity.

Why not hear it straight from the source:

*Tumblr lets you effortlessly **share anything**. Post text, photos, quotes, links, music, and videos, from your browser, phone, desktop, email, or wherever you happen to be. You can **customize everything**, from colors, to your theme's HTML.*

Search for bloggers sharing music similar to yours, follow them, reblog and favorite their posts, and let the networking begin.

I find myself spending more time **ReBlogging** videos, news, and downloads from blogs I follow than I do actual blogging of my own content. Reblogging is:

The same way YouTube embeds make it easy for a video to become a viral hit, the "reblog" button on all Tumblr posts allows a meme to spread rapidly across thousands of blogs with just a click.

Podomatic is a podcasting platform.

The free accounts come with limited space, but you can always delete the outdated podcasts to upload new ones.

The reason I mention this one is because I receive a non-stop stream of friend adds from this service.

Even if its only 1 a day, I am replying and following new podcasters daily.

This definitely makes it a valuable resource for expanding your fanbase.

Blip.fm is very similar to Twitter but it turns every user into a DJ.

Search for a song and Blip it.

What is a blip you say?

A blip is a combination of 1) a song and 2) a short message that accompanies it. The way you create a blip is to first search for a song that you want to hear (or a song that you want your listeners to hear), then add a short message (under 150 characters), finally you submit it.

As you begin favoriting other DJs, you have the ability to ReBlip as well as give Props to the songs others are sharing.

There is also a feature to Blip your own media.

To add to the punch, you are able to connect Blip.fm to your Twitter account so all the music you share is also seen by your Twitter followers.

Mixcloud is more visually appealing than podomatic and also allows you to separate your podcasts into tracks.

For these two reasons, I have to be honest and say that I prefer Mixcloud to Podomatic (but both are valuable networking resources).

Groups is a new feature recently released and since it rolled out I have noticed an increase in activity on my account.

However, the traffic does not compare to the daily adds and follows from Podomatic.

I have always been a big fan of Soundcloud.

The feature that stands out the most is the ability to leave comments on a track while it is playing.

Your comment is even timestamped and appears at the point in the song where you actually typed it.

Although hosting space is limited unless you pay, it is still a great place to build a network of like minded music fanatics.

Finding music similar to your own or discovering that hot new indie artist and interacting with them has never been easier.

Music Marketing Tips

- Search for other users by genre. Also find people who share your influences or have music tastes similar to your own.
- Do NOT limit your networking to music-only blogs, groups, and networks.
- When you aren't making music, what books do you read? what movies do you watch? do you garden? are you a parent? are you a studio tech geek?
- Finding blogs and other potential fans who are interested in the same topics you are is another way to find people who might like your music. One of these people could be your next #1 fan.
- Its safe to assume a large percentage of people who read parenting blogs are also music lovers. I know a few people who enjoy meditation music while gardening or doing yoga.
- Podcasting and internet radio are very similar entities. Never underestimate the power of having your new single featured during popular podcasts. These networks are also prime places to run into radio station personnel. Just

like you, many stations are using social media and podcasting to market themselves and engage with their audiences.

- Thank people who follow or fan you, and return the favor. If they comment on your music, listen to theirs and comment back.
- There is no such thing as overnight success. It is a slow, steady, daily process and the only way to move forward is to **do something**.

Social Media Tools for Bands, Musicians, And Everyone Else – part i

Either I have tested these and found them helpful or currently use them on a regular basis.

TweetDeck

Tweetdeck is so sweet Twitter paid $40 million+ for it back in May.

Consider this fine piece of coding your social media control center.

This little puppy grants you access to your accounts on Twitter, Myspace, Linked-In, Foursquare, as well as the ability to tie into WordPress and Tumblr using APIs.

Below is an excerpt from the desktop client feature list found on their website. You can download clients for your desktop, iPhone, Android, or grab the extension for Chrome browsers.

- *Update Twitter, Facebook, MySpace, LinkedIn, Google Buzz and Foursquare*
- *Retweet Twitter style – or your style*
- *Check-in to Foursquare direct from the client*
- *Manage conversations with @replies and direct messages*
- *Keep your finger on the pulse with MySpace*
- *View YouTube videos within TweetDeck, and record and share video clips though TwitVid*
- *Manage multiple Twitter accounts easily*
- *Use our scheduling feature to check-in or send a tweet in the future*
- *See what's hot with Twitter Trends and*
- *Organize and update Facebook with TweetDeck*
- *Follow topics in real-time with saved searches, editable from within the column*
- *Add, create and manage Twitter Lists*
- *Use your TweetDeck Account to add all of your social network accounts in one go*
- *Keep your TweetDeck safe with sync and back-up*
- *Avoid Twitter spam with TweetDeck's spam button*
- *Share and view photos with support for Flickr, Twitgoo and mobypicture*
- *Use keyboard shortcuts to speed up your messaging*

Video: http://www.youtube.com/watch**?v=PEDOXHEfxrw**

Pledge Music

PledgeMusic.com is a service that integrates your social media accounts into a platform that allows artists to provide exclusive content to their fans while allowing the fans to pledge (or donate) money to the recording projects, music video shoots, or other reasons their favorite band might need funding to move their career forward.

By providing the platform to create such a unique experience with your fan base, Pledge Music is a win-win situation.

The only way you could lose is by not having any fans donating to your project.

In the words of the team of geniuses behind this service:

You are your own A&R and Marketing Manager – you choose the studio, the producer, the artwork, the promotion – it's all down to you! Let the fans be your label, while you keep the rights to your music.

Headliner.fm

Headliner.fm puts your social media reach on steroids.

And it's simple:

1. Sign-up
2. Connect your Twitter, Facebook, and/or Myspace accounts
3. Invite friends and Recommend others' promotions
4. Earn Band Bucks and use them to create your own promotions
5. Repeat

As an example, my latest campaign ran from October 23 until November 7 and was seen over 40,000 times and shared by over 15 different users of the Headliner.fm service.

And that's only 1 example out of many.

A very clever and useful service you definitely want to put to use.

They also offer premium features to paying members including in-depth analytics and the ability to repeat promotions without doing any extra work.

Video: http://www.youtube.com/watch?v=OPsJ3qJY7SU

Buying Fans, SEO, and Social Proof – On First Listen – Google Plus HOA Panel Discussion

Unfortunately I was not able to make it in time for our discussion panel concerning buying fans, black hat vs white hat SEO, and social proof as it applies to online music marketing.

In an attempt to continue the discussion and contribute my 2 cents, you can read my thoughts below the video.

But first, here are the details about this week's episode:

In this Special edition of On First Listen, sponsored by the Google Plus Music Professionals Community, we brought in a panel of music and video promotion experts and geeks to discuss the pitfalls and advantages of "black hat" SEO versus "organic" search engine optimization. "Social Proof" – the indication of value by follow and share numbers – also played a role in the conversation.

Mark Ferrasci, Debra Russell, Diane Cobb, Matthias Schaller, Richard Wildman, and Ronnie Bincer share their expertise and advice for the Mid Tenn audience.

I don't know of any other video on the net that openly discusses these topics in a way that will be of value to independent musicians, artists, or promoters.

YouTube and Buying Views

Let's face it. Majority of online marketers are buying views. What happens to your YouTube account depends on how you go about doing it.

In reference to the screenshot below – using Google Adwords I was able to generate 335 views at an average cost-per-view of 15 cents. The majority of the views which counted toward the total view count were delivered via YouTube's in-stream ads (which play before you watch a video on YouTube – "you can skip this ad in 5..4..3...).

In other words, people (in our target market) were forced to watch the video for at least 5 seconds which YouTube then counts toward your view count.

Their recent move of suspending accounts and stripping views has as much to do with their profits as it does with delivering quality search results to their users.

Using Virool, I can purchase views for 9 cents each. And YouTube does not flag, warn, or block you for these.

With that said, buying views is not the issue.

How you buy them is the problem.

White Hat vs Black Hat

For clarity's sake...

White hat leaves you in good graces with the gods of YouTube and the other companies currently upgrading their defenses against spam. This is known as following community guidelines and actually reading through the terms of service.

You can use Twitter Ads to "buy followers". I need to clarify, you are not necessarily paying them for followers – you are paying Twitter to show your account to more people (in your target market) and label it as a Promoted Account. ...but then again, since you are only charged when someone "clicks", you are essentially paying for a follower. This is the same as running Facebook Ads. You are essentially "buying likes".

Black hat refers to the methods and techniques used to "game the system". Also known as buying views, followers, or fans that are typically not real people.

This comes in the form of buying 10,000 Twitter followers for $10 from a company (selling fake accounts) or purchasing back-links to your website in an attempt to rank on the front page of Google.

Social Proof

When this topic originally started as a discussion in our G+ Music Professionals community, the concept of social proof quickly became the focus.

At about 17:00 in the above video, Ronnie Bincer makes some great points about social proof.

Admit it. When you search for a video on YouTube and skim through the list of results; you naturally gravitate toward the one with the most views.

If everyone else watched this one, it has to the be the [best/correct] one.

I do it.

Social proof is how we determine the quality, validity, or popularity of music, products, or services.

This is what leads people to boost their numbers as quickly as possible. I have experimented with black hat services and other services I consider "gray hat" to gain followers, Likes, or views. I have even tried services that boost Likes, Favorites, Subscriptions, and Comments on your YouTube account.

Despite how many followers, views, likes, fans, or plays you have on your content – it means nothing if no one is engaging with you, visiting your website (repeatedly), or sharing/buying your music. 10,000 dead bodies does NOTHING for your music or building it into a sustainable income.

Spammers operate on the theory that if they can put their product in front of 1,000,000 people – 1% will buy. 1% of 1 million is a nice chunk of change.

This is a valid point. Performing at a music festival in front of thousands of people will help you find more fans quicker than playing a show at the dingy bar down the street.
Now let me make another point.

If you are a hip hop group playing at an americana festival – the likelihood of you gaining new fans is slim to none.

The issue then becomes **relevance** which is a significant factor in this discussion of social proof and online music marketing. Black hat methods and services do not provide targeted marketing campaigns. They simply spam by any means necessary. Spamming annoys people, gets you ignored, or worse – blocked.

When you advertise through Google Adwords (Twitter or Facebook), you are able to precisely target your efforts by location, keywords, interests, and other factors.

This is possible because **the one with the most data wins** – Facebook knows everything about everybody and their pets so naturally they will use advertising to profit from it.

Conclusion

Specifically in music, you need to swallow your pride and do it the hard way like every other classic band that came before you.

Organic growth, grass roots movements, street team organizations, and simply busting your ass day and night to promote your next show. This is how you build a quality, worthwhile, engaged fan base.

Your metrics for social proof need to include the more important things such as 1) fan engagement – comments, likes, shares, RTs, 2) event attendance, and 3) album and merch sales.

Numbers do nothing if they are just numbers.

Why NOT To Buy YouTube Views

I have said it over and over again to so many people...

But people tend to not listen.

Here is what happens if you buy YouTube views from sites selling them by the tens of thousands for dirt cheap (or any other automated form of number boosting).

Numbers do NOT equal fans.

Watch and learn. And don't forget, I told you so.

Regarding your account: ▮▮▮▮▮▮▮▮▮▮

This following video was found in Violation of TOU #4 Section H:

▮▮▮▮▮▮▮▮▮▮▮▮▮▮▮▮▮▮▮▮▮▮

http://www.youtube.com/t/terms

"You agree not to use or launch any automated system, including without limitation, "robots," "spiders," or "offline readers," that accesses the Service in a manner that sends more request messages to the YouTube servers in a given period of time than a human can reasonably produce in the same period by using a conventional on-line web browser. Notwithstanding the foregoing, YouTube grants the operators of public search engines permission to use spiders to copy materials from the site for the sole purpose of and solely to the extent necessary for creating publicly available searchable indices of the materials, but not caches or archives of such materials. YouTube reserves the right to revoke these exceptions either generally or in specific cases. You agree not to collect or harvest any personally identifiable information, including account names, from the Service, nor to use the communication systems provided by the Service (e.g., comments, email) for any commercial solicitation purposes. You agree not to solicit, for commercial purposes, any users of the Service with respect to their Content."

Please note that your video content has been removed. You may reupload your removed videos in such a way that is not violative of our TOU.

Should your account be found in violation of our Terms of Use #4 Section H again, your account will be suspended without the possibility for appeal.

YouTube takes the abuse of its system very seriously. Any user found gaming views, subscribers, meta-data or otherwise misleading users will have their account statistics wiped on the first offense, and on the second offense have their account permanently terminated.

Many users trust their account to outside marketers who claim to be able to increase views, etc. You are responsible for activity that happens on your account, and are responsible for knowing and abiding by our terms - this means understanding the nature of the traffic on your channel and making sure you are in compliance with our terms.

Sincerely,
The YouTube Team

How To Improve Your Google Search Results

People (a lot of them) use Google daily for exploring the web and finding information.

What most people do not understand is the "mostly unknown" complexities of searching the web with Google.

Allow me to introduce a few tips for improving your search results.

Google Search Basics

Most people simply type their phrase into the search box, how to use google search, but there are several tricks you can use to improve your results. Let's start with the basic ones.

Exact Words, Exact Phrases

By using "quotation marks" around your search term(s), you are telling Google to return results including that exact "word" or "exact phrase".

Going along with our screenshot above for the phrase **tennessee music**, let's see what happens when we search for **"tennessee music"** (in quotes).

Notice how the results changed and now include sites where the words Tennessee and Music are used together.

Related Words and Synonyms

Using a tilde (~) is the opposite of using quotes for exact matches.
Searching ~crackers returns any results that are related to crackers including hackers, cracks, cracking, Keebler.

This OR That

You can also use OR to return results using one term or the other.

Searching twitter OR youtube will show you pages related to either Twitter or YouTube. Another example would be advertising OR promotion.

The OR has to be capitalized.

Excluding Words

If I wanted to search for "tennessee music" but do not want to see any results related to UT Knoxville, I could use the minus (-) sign to exclude words from my search.
Below are the results for **"tennessee music" -knoxville**.

Site Search

Google allows you to search within a specific site using the site: modifier.

If I wanted to search "social media" only within www.midtnmusic.com then I would type this in the search box: **site:midtnmusic.com "social media"**.

If you only wanted results about "social media" from academic sources, you could search like this: **site:.edu "social media"**.

Google will only return results about social media from websites with .edu domains.

Specific Document Types

If you are trying to find specific file types, you can use the modifier filetype: to locate PDFs or powerpoint presentations.

Searching **"online music marketing" filetype:pd**f returns the following:

More Search Tips and Tricks

Here are a few more tricks for getting more out of your Google search results.

Definitions

To find the definition of a word simply search: **define:hippopotamus**.

Calculator

No need to go through the steps of opening the calculator program that came installed on your computer.

Simply use the Google search box to find the answer. **5234 * 3432 / 12**

Conversions

Need to know how many pints are in a gallon? Simply search for **pints to gallons** or **5 pints in gallons**.

Area Codes and Phone Listings

If you simply type in the 3-digit area code, Google will tell you what area is represented.

If someone calls you and you want to find out who it was, simply search for **phonebook:1-555-555-5555**.

Stocks

Enter a ticker symbol (GOOG) and Google will show you the current financial information related to those specific stocks.

Numeric Ranges

If you were looking for information that included a specific range of numbers or info related to a specific period in history, then simply search **online marketing 1990..2000** or **music industry 1960..1970**.

Resources

- **Tips & Tricks** by Google Inside Search
- How To Search Google Like A Pro: 11 Tricks You Have To Know via HowToGeek.com
- 12 Quick Tips To Search Google Like An Expert via Hubspot.com
- How to Search Google Like a Pro (infographic) via ApexPacific.com

3 Absolute Musts For Website SEO, How to Keep it Simple

What Must you do to Optimize your site for Search Engines?

I'm going to jump right in assuming you at least know what the letters SEO mean to the web, if you don't, go set up your **Google Webmaster Tools,** read the intro, and come right on back over here. We'll take the approach that your site has yet to be built, but understand that is seldom the real case, and these things can be done at any time and should be updated frequently.

Step 1: Think and Write

Think about your site's **purpose,** think about who you want to find your site, think about what is going to be avilable on your site. **Think about your site like a visitor to your site.**

Write down your thoughts. Name the pages, jot down the information and format in a sketch and underline the words that pop up most often. These will be your first "keywords".

Now use those **webmaster tools** and learn about some more possible keywords and phrases. All the while Think about your site as if you are a visitor, and select things that are popularly searched and fit very well with your site. Write them down.

Joshua Smotherman gives a great primer on keywords in Keyword Research 101: Why Are We Writing So Many Articles About ReverbNation?

Step 2: Populate your site

Once you have your keywords and your page texts written, edited, proofed, edited, and proofed again, it is time to populate the proper fields within the background code of the site itself. It's only slightly technical, and more than half of it is done for you if you properly use WordPress or another of the many fine Content Management Systems (CMS) available.

You will be listing the "keywords" into the "meta data" of the <head> section of the <html>. Sounds hard, it's not. The meta data is the part that tells the "internet" that your site exists and all the helpful bits about it, so that people can find it.

Now, if you don't have a clue at this point, get help! If you feel like you can handle it, learn your HTML tricks where I learn mine.

Step 3: Make sure your site map is indexed.

Again, it's a simple task with WordPress or any other CMS, and just a bit of code in HTML. What you are doing is telling the spiders and crawlers of the search engines what is on your site. It may seem obvious to some, but it's an often missed element, and what good is a beautifully implemented SEO strategy if the web doesn't know the site exists, eh?

Bonus Tips!

- GoTo the top and read the first tip again. Keep the human element in mind all the time.
- Google indexes every word. Not Just Keywords! They check phrases for meanings... see what I'm driving at?

You want to write in a way that keeps your readers interested and has the right keywords, but don't go hog-wild! Use of simile and hyperbole and all the good literary tips is a Good thing.

- Up-to-date content is also very important. It is for this reason that most experts suggest keeping a blog. Post something new each week at a minimum. When you start doing this, going into the site's servers and uploading new pages all slicked out with the keywords and all the little tags and what-not gets to be a right pain in the butt.

That's why you use WordPress… When I finish typing, here in this box, I'll click in the next one and fill in the title, description, keywords and tags, hit the publish button, and I'm done!

One last goody: Make sure you take advantage of Google's "Authorship" markup. It's a little tricky to set up, but worth it. You may have noticed that when you search for things on Google, you see more things that have a person's picture and G+ link with them.

Rel="Author": How To Implement Google Authorship Markup

These people have utilized the rel=author tag to link their writing to their google profile.

This gives credibility to the credible and provides proof of ownership to the original author. Neat, huh? As you begin to trust sources, you begin to recognize their picture, and google notices that you read a lot from writer "x" thus they know to include that source in relevant searches.

Golden Nugget:

If you use the Genesis Framework for WordPress, all you need to do to complete Google Authorship is copy and paste the URL of your Google+ profile to the Google+ box on your profile in the WordPress Dashboard. On your Google+ profile page, add your website URL as a site you contribute to and you are good to go.

How To Set Up Twitter Ads And Get Your Music Heard

Tutorial Video:

http://www.youtube.com/watch?v=gCVcoEZCER4

Twitter recently launched their advertising platform to small businesses.

By setting a daily budget and a cost-per-follow for **promoted accounts** and cost-per-click for **promoted tweets**, you are able to inexpensively and effectively target Twitter users locally or globally.

In the above how to video, I demonstrate how to set up your Twitter Ads account to begin promoting your music online.

Here is a quick run-down of the steps:

1. log in with your Twitter account
2. enter your payment information

3. choose locations (country, state, province) you wish to target

4. for promoted account, set your daily budget and cost-per-follow

5. for promoted tweets, set your daily budget, cost-per-click, and choose which Tweets you wish to promote or allow Twitter to choose for you

Twitter Ad Positions - Non-Mobile Web

If you have noticed the yellow arrow and Promoted next to Tweets and Accounts, this is Twitter Ads in action.

Twitter Ads - Positions In Mobile App

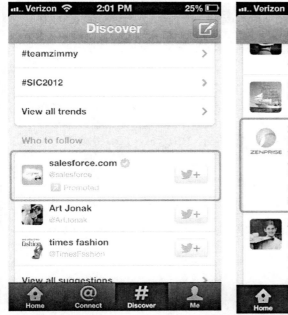 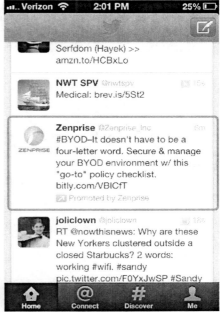

This is where Promoted Accounts appear in Twitter Mobile Ads.

This is how Twitter Ads Promoted Tweets appear on mobile apps.

Notes and Quick Tips

Have a goal, stick to the plan.

You must have a game plan.

Do NOT target the entire world and let your money drain away without results.

Determine a primary goal (ex: drive traffic to album buy link) and focus your Promoted Tweets on driving traffic to links where people can purchase your music (Amazon, iTunes, CD Baby, your website).

Change campaigns weekly or monthly if you need to. The important tip here is to not waste money promoting useless Tweets.

Make sure you are putting thought behind what you are promoting and where you are sending the traffic.

Food for thought about Promoted Accounts

When using Promoted Accounts to pay for followers, consider the fact that the majority of Twitter users follow people in hopes to gain a follow back (#teamfollowback ring a bell?).

I guarantee you will pay for followers who will unfollow in a few days when you do not follow back. [If you are someone who follows everyone back, disregard this message.]
Think about this when considering your budget.

If you have a brand new Twitter account, you will want to target locally or regionally (especially if you play shows). This will help you find people to interact with.

If you have hundreds or thousands of followers, the chances of you paying for useless follows will increase significantly. I have already seen this occur on a campaign I recently completed for a hip hop group.

We decided to disable the promoted account feature 2 days into the campaign and focus solely on driving traffic to the music through promoted tweets.

Promoted Tweets

A few things to remember to get the most bang for your buck:

- Include links that matter: your website, album purchase links, youtube video links, features or reviews on blogs
- If you are touring or playing shows regionally, update your location settings daily in order to spend money targeting the area you will be playing your next show. Make sure most of your Promoted Tweets include links to

a blog post or event listing including details about the show. Photos of show flyers are fair game.

What Are Hashtags and How To Use Them

I am going to assume you have seen a **#hashtag** before...even if you are not sure where they came from or their purpose.

Allow me to provide some insight.

What are hashtags?

According to Twitter:

The # symbol, called a hashtag, is used to mark keywords or topics in a Tweet. It was created organically by Twitter users as a way to categorize messages.

But it is important to understand they **existed long before Twitter** and are not a creation of their's or of the Twitter community.

In fact, hashtags were first seen in IRCs (Internet Relay Chat) which were created in 1988.

Their purpose was to label groups or topics and to mark individual messages as relevant to a specific channel. Their use on Twitter was a natural result of their use in IRC channels.

You can learn more from Wikipedia about the history of hashtags and IRCs.

How do I use them?

Can I create my own?

Yes and it is simple. When on Twitter, Google+, Instagram, or other network that uses them, place a # in front of a word or phrase with #nospaces. Once you enter a space or other character that is not a letter, the hashtag breaks.

How are they useful?

In the below screenshot notice how many of the trending topics on Twitter consist of #hashtags. 6 out of 10 or 60% (if I counted correctly).

Only the most popular topics appear in this list so a lot of people have to be using those hashtags for them to become trending.

With that said, whether on Twitter or G+, use hashtags in the search box to find like-minded individuals. For instance #Music101, #Parenting, or #FF (follow friday).

Here is a list of ideas for using hashtags:

- find people to follow.
- find news or follow events.
- start conversations or get involved in existing discussions.
- brand your album, event, or new single.
- make it easy for users to find your band by creating a custom, easy-to-remember hashtag.
- run a contest or other marketing campaign and use hashtags to track sharing and other activity.

What are some tips for using hashtags?

Keep them short and relevant. Typically one word or short phrases like #IGotAThingFor.

Use them to search for groups of people that share your interests. Searching for genres (#hiphop) or phrases like

#newmusic or #indiemusic can help you find others to follow and connect with.

Specifically on Twitter, including #nowplaying or #video when Tweeting your songs or videos can potentially put your links in front of more people.

Organize campaigns around your new album or an upcoming gig by creating a hashtag specific to each event. Use your existing fans and your mailing list to make your hashtags popular.

I have included some useful links below.

Resources

- What Are Hashtags? via Twitter Help
- Hashtag via Wikipedia
- Internet Relay Chat via Wikipedia
- Quick Start Guide to Hashtags via Hashtags.org
- How To Use Hashtags on Twitter: A Simple Guide for Marketers via Hubspot
- How To Use Hashtags Without Looking Like A Total Beginner via Technorati

Hashtags for Google+ and YouTube

Hashtags, those nearly ubiquitous, but mostly misunderstood # signs you see all over Twitter, YouTube, G+ and so many other places, even Facebook (but they don't work there). **How do you use them?** Oh, you don't? You should. But, *how?*

Well, before we get started, if you are a total newb to hashtags, or want a deeper look at how they began and are commonly used, be sure to read the jedi's article, "What Are Hashtags and How To Use Them".

As Joshua said,

Here is a list of ideas for using hashtags:

- find people to follow.
- find news or follow events.
- start conversations or get involved in existing discussions.
- brand your album, event, or new single.

- make it easy for users to find your band by creating a custom, easy-to-remember hashtag.
- run a contest or other marketing campaign and use hashtags to track sharing and other activity.

Hashtags for G+ and YouTube search

A couple fellas were lamenting their struggles using Search on G+, today, which is what eventually brought me to add this post. I've picked up a tip or two from some very helpful people, and sharing them is what I like to do. So, let's do a little "How To on Google Hashtags."

Topics, Pictures, People, Pages and more...

Google not only references every word typed into G+ and YouTube, but they also keep up with the hashtags for us. You can search by words and phrases, or you can use hashtags and get completely different results. Try this.

1. Put the words "Jedi Hashtag" into the search bar on G+, note your results
2. Change it to "#jedihashtag", note your results

Fine tune your results

- "Nashville Live Music" serves too broad a scope? **Use multiple hashtags in search with commas between.** #nashville, #live, #country, #events will serve things tagged with those words.
- Use the dropdown menu to choose what type of results are shown. Choose "From You" to see posts You made with the hashtag of your choice.

Keep track of your own stuff (medicine for the headache)

- If you share lots of automobile photos (for example), try hashtagging the make and year, then if you need that post of the cool #73mustang you did six months ago, it's a second away!
- Use them in your video descriptions and they are not only more visible in search, but it makes it very easy to keep up with playlists of your favorite topics and to sort your own videos.
- Use them in private or limited share posts within your company to keep track of #productionnotes or #AerofoilDesignIdea, for example.

These are a few of the jedi practices that have streamlined my daily internet adventures and helped me to be productive. If you have a #jedihashtag #tip , why not share it with us?

George Miller of www.gminteractive.com has been helping lots of folks learn the hashtag tricks on his show "Let's Talk About It," which airs daily at 10 am PST. Find it on plus ... search #gminteractive

Oh, speaking of that, did you notice the swank new button above the comments section? It lets you comment and use the site as a logged in member without the bother of all that signing up stuff! And yes, it's only available for **G+ users.**

Keep making awesome music and art, and keep on plussin'. over and out.

How To Create An Attractive Profile

Part two of the series, "Your Your Social Profile is Your Resume"

There are many schools of thought on what's important in a social profile, or even *if* it's important. What if you are in the indie music business (or want to be)? Do you think it's a good idea to try to promote your work without a visible public profile to let folk know who you are (or that you are at least a real person)? I don't, and neither do the professionals I have talked with about it.

In part one of this series, we talked about pictures and how they represent so much on-line. All of our contacts agreed that a clear photo of yourself can greatly increase your chances of making new connections.

But, what about all those other "boxes"? Do you really need to fill out all that stuff? Well, in a word, yes. But what should be there? What shouldn't? See what some professionals think, and let us know your thoughts.

Before we get into the thick of it, as you know, I don't just launch into this stuff on a whim; I do my research and hopefully, that's what you are doing. I was surprised when I searched for tips and advice on creating an attractive and professional public social profile. Two things came up: SEO for LinkedIn and how to make an on-line dating profile attractive.

A Note on Linked-In: LinkedIn is intended for use by professionals. So, a complete profile is imperative. This is definitely a "resume" oriented profile. No BS, and good grammar are very important. You also need to be aware that if you join LinkedIn and start sending a bunch of strangers or loose connections those same old "Check out my song" messages, you are going to Piss People Off. Period. This ain't the old My-Space.

So, what's the most important part of your public profile?

I talked with a few people about the importance of a public profile and all agreed that in the professional world, complete and accurate information is a must.

In the first part of this series, we talked about the importance of a good picture. This week we'll look at the details and what should be included for public view.

They say the devil is in the details, so make sure you leave him out of yours. An appropriate profile picture is essential, but it does not tell your story. When you reach out to connect with someone on the net, it is the information that you make public which influences whether your invitation is accepted.

Richard Wildman of Music Scene Investigation receives hundreds of such invitations each month. He doesn't have time to do a forensic search to decide who is on the level, so like the rest of us, he has to make an informed decision quickly.

Richard Wildman I have to admit that my profile isn't as good as it could be. That being said I think that profiles are important as a first impression. Secondarily, it is my belief that the introduction is more important than photos. However, I believe that content is the most telling aspect as way of introduction/intent.

As this topic has to do with the profile, Introduction is where I look before determining if one is added to my circles.

Rich has a valid point. Your picture could be of anyone. The short intro or "tagline" is your first opportunity to give the world an attractive impression of yourself. This is where those keywords come in handy, especially in the case that someone may actually be searching for someone just like You! If you don't understand the basic concept of "keywords" and "seo," you owe it to yourself to read a little more.

Well known business coach, Debra Russell of Artists-Edge, is on top of this one, and here is her advice:

Debra Russell *I think the thing people don't think about enough is who is their target market and what are the key words they're searching for. So, if you can sprinkle in your target market's key words, they are much more likely to find you. And isn't that the point – that the right people find you?*

In fact everyone I have spoken with is in agreement that it's the details that count. What information is in your profile? What should be there? Do you think it makes a difference whether you are socializing just for fun or on a professional basis?

Regardless your original intent, there is a decent chance that your professional colleagues, employers, or potential employers may cruise your page for some reason, so it's always smart to make sure you at least don't look the part of the fool. A good friend in HR for a multi-national auto company described in painful detail the hassles he deals with because of the insanity that some employees and applicants post publicly. Trust me, you don't want the company investigating your politics just because a co-worker didn't like the picture you posted with a beer and a hunting rifle while bitching about the job. And they don't want to deal with it, either!

So, with a good head-shot, and an attractive by-line, what's next? Details, details, details.

Most of the social networks public and private follow a similar theme in profile information. So in the "big box" that asks for details, is where you get down to the nitty-gritty.

- You want to present a complete and accurate descritption, but this is not where you do the whole life-story thing, okay? You want to introduce yourself much like you would with a new friend or on an interview.

- Professional background is important, of course and if you want to attract like-minded people you should include a few of your interests or passions. Notice I didn't say, "turn-ons."
- You will also want to provide links to your other sites and profiles.
- You might give some personal or geographic background. It can be very helpful, but again, we're not writing a book.

Most sites offer special slots for current employment, phone, email, address, etc. Now, these are the really touchy subjects from the personal point of view.

How do you handle that? I mean, you do want serious pros to be able to reach you, but you don't want just anyone ringing you up in the middle of a meeting. Well, that's where the tricky little privacy settings come in handy.

- For email, use a dedicated email through your site or google, such as "bob@bobsbusiness.com" or "yourbusiness@gmail.com". This should be publicly available. Keep a personal account for your family and friends, and use a business account for serious business.
- On the phone scene, I am a huge fan of Google Talk or Voice (whatever it's called this week). You can create a free voice-over-ip phone number through Google and forward it to your cell, or use it when on-line only. It's a great option if you don't have an actual office or business

phone. Keep this one open to "friends." You can decide later who to give your personal numbers to.

- Don't publish your personal address publicly. Storefront businesses should have a public address. Giving your general location (city,state) is a nice touch.
- As far as Big Brother goes, well, get over it, or get off the net... he's got you pegged, regardless.

I hope this helps you determine what to put in your profile. In part three, we'll discuss some ideas for keeping things organized and easy to access, as well as how to leverage SEO from Google, WordPress and Gravatar to make certain that people can find the *right* you.

Expand Your Fan Base: Jump In My Social Media Time Machine

The Post-World War II economic expansion led to the explosion of American suburbs and the classic Leave It To Beaver imagery.

A television in every home. More time for leisure led to more screen time which gave advertisers more opportunity to tap your brain.

Even before television there was radio, door-to-door salesmen...one could even argue that advertising began in the golden days of rock art.

Although some say marketing is a young discipline; others say it has existed since the first buyers and sellers developed the concept of a marketplace. This would include non-monetary exchanges such as barter and trade which still happens more than we tend to realize.

The point is that most of us have been programmed by a world full of commercial broadcast messages. Growing up with multiple TVs in the home, multiple screens in every bar, and now movies stream to the phones in our pockets; how is it possible to avoid?

Imagine a time...

There was a very hefty chunk of human history when we survived in small family units and lived with the land.

Obviously something happened and we multiplied...

Along the way it became clear that some of us were really skilled with cattle and some of us grew amazing tomatoes.

Now if I grew amazing tomatoes but I loved steak, I'm pretty sure I would find the guy with the best cattle and offer him some juicy eats in exchange for a thick T-bone.

With that said, I believe...

Social Media is taking us back

Every day I witness the power Social Media is giving back to individuals as well as their tribes (or in this case, fan base).

Each new artist we work with strengthens my belief that we are tuning out traditional broadcast messages. We now have full control of filtering what we consume.

Instead of settling for 1-way communication (TV, radio, and satellite), we log-in and search for what we want or ask those closest to us for their recommendations and opinions.

We also have the power to create our own content and share it. Not only with our close friends but the entire globe...in just a few clicks.

*If your content sucks or you just like to yell at people demanding attention, **we simply turn you off and move on**.*

When you follow someone on Twitter, friend them on Facebook, or fan them on ReverbNation, in essence, you are knocking on their door and shaking their hand hoping to grab their attention with enough force to get 'em hooked.

Simply put, how good are your *social* skills?

Do you know:

- Who your ideal fan is?
- What they read?
- What they watch?
- How they buy music?
- Where do they hang out?
- Are they religious?

If you do, it's highly probable you already know which tribe(s) you belong to.

I happen to be a father, husband, hip hop head, songwriter, blogger, social media geek...you get the idea.

What's the point?

As the major labels and the rest of the music industry are still getting a grip on peer-to-peer file sharing, the Internet and technology in general; the music business is going back to what it used to be...

Passionate people that love music and work for little pay to simply help inspiring talent take it to the next level.

It's that hard rock band from down the block who sleep in a run-down van surviving off one meal a day going city to city booking gigs while they drive.

It's that aspiring songwriter who puts her heart and soul into her YouTube channel everyday waiting for someone to notice and leave a comment.

It's you, it's me, it's us.

As independent labels and artists continue educating themselves on the power of marketing via the web, it solidifies the fact that have to have a team to make it.

Manager, booking agent, publisher, your website guy, your street team, your mailing list, and every single fan are all necessary elements for a healthy music career.

Even the guy who stands in the back corner at your local shows but talks sh** about you on his blog contributes to the efforts..

Ally with other tribes for exponential growth

Now that you have the ability to introduce yourself to just about anyone, I suggest you do it.

If you found an amazing punk band and you feel this band is the perfect fit for sharing the stage next to you on your upcoming small tour...

What's stopping you from contacting them and finding out more about their schedule and if they are interested in swapping gigs? In return, you can book a show in your city and provide them a place to stay when they are there.

If that band has a loyal following and you make music their fans will enjoy, chances are your fan base can grow significantly overnight.

...and Collaborate

I receive messages quite often from artists asking about collab opportunities. On the flip side, we also send messages to other artists to discuss our own collaboration ideas.

The fastest way to put your talent in front of a brand new audience is to collaborate with others who already have one.

It's a win-win for both because you gain exposure to their tribe and they gain exposure to yours.

Remember...

The days of shoving advertisements in our face in order to sell units are dwindling.

Social Media gives us the ability to build our own tribes and ally with other tribes in order to develop our own economies.

You have to know what tribe(s) you belong to, how to get the attention of those people, and how to give them what they are searching for.

If you do not take the time to introduce yourself, demand too much attention, or your content sucks, your marketing will be unsuccessful.

Content includes songs, videos, stories from the road, photos from your last show, or merchandise. You can also provide gear reviews, share your recording process when you're in the studio, or review albums from other bands in your genre.

Content is what you use to engage your audience so it is imperative that you create to the best of your abilities.

After you have achieved this, it's all a matter of maintaining a tribal mentality as you grow.

Think small, grow big.

Is Your Music Career Running On Cheap Gas?

Originally published by Jedi Bret on the Small Barn site.

Out in the county, where the gas stations are few and far between, I looked at the gas gauge, and sure enough the needle was right down there on the Empty peg. Typical...

My old Ford has been abused for a couple decades and she gets pretty noisy. Rattles and pings, valves clacking, and is that an exhaust leak or something worse? She keeps on going, though, so I give her a quart of oil every now and then and figure I'll get her to the health clinic as soon as possible.

Now, I try to stick to No Ethanol fuel. If you think that stuff is good for your car, find a no-ethanol station, and switch for 2 weeks – I dare you. I'm also a firm believer in running higher octane fuel, especially in newer engines (ask the race pros).

Better fuel wins races.

So, there I was, out of gas, and looking forward to those out-in-the-county prices, when I see the sign at Summitville is marked only 4¢ higher than in town. Yay! I noticed one, hard to get to, pump that says 0% ethanol, and headed that way.

As I parked I saw it was 90 octane, an added bonus, even though it was another 4¢ more. I got $14 worth, (almost bought some fried chicken livers – gotta love country stores) and headed on my way.

Pulling onto the highway, the Bronco sounded and felt a little different. I played around with the accelerator, and noticed the pinging was gone, the stutter was a better, the noises that make one think, "is this thing going to make it?" were just not there.

I finished my chores for the day and headed back to the house. When I arrived home, there was still gas in the tank. I expected it to be empty, again, as it normally would be after that drive. But that wasn't the case. Yesterday's mileage on the good fuel had left me with enough to send the wife off to work today, knowing that she had enough gas to get through her day!

Are you promoting your music on low-grade fuel?

Find out by continuing the article on Small Barn Sound's website: www.smallbarnsound.com

4 Reasons Why Your Band Needs To Blog

If you have a website, but you are not actively maintaining a blog...

You are seriously killing your marketing game.

Let's dive in.

1. Search Engine Optimization (SEO)

One of the most popular questions I am asked:

"How do I get my website on the front page of Google?"
It's not easy.

One of the most significant factors considered when ranking websites in search results is the freshness of your content.

If you built your website 6 months ago and have not updated it since, forget about it.

Blogging at least once a week can considerably increase your chances at ranking higher in search results.

Other factors include:

- relevance of your content.
- are you a reputable blogger with a loyal following (this is starting to play a bigger role).
- keywords and key phrases found inside your content.
- meta titles, descriptions, and keywords.
- are you using h1 and h2 heading tags in your content?
- images, captions, and meta information.
- other websites including links back to yours.
- do you have a Facebook Page? are you on Twitter? signed up for Google+ yet?

That is not the full list but this article is about blogging, not SEO.

2. Blog, Engage

Your #1 goal (no matter what) should be to drive all web traffic to www.yourbandname.com. You should then aim to engage with visitors.

You want them to 1) click play, 2) join your mailing list, 3) buy your music, and (most importantly) 4) engage with you.

It is one thing to say that, but it is a completely different monster to pull it off effectively.

Blogs (no matter what platform) are designed for community discussion. That's why all blogs have a built-in comments system.

Even if you choose not to put any emphasis on blog comments, you can still use each blog post to entice fans to consume and share your content.

Blogging is how you keep current fans coming back. It also increases your chances at connecting with new fans.

In order to engage people, you need to have great content. Keep reading for examples and ideas.

3. Share, Spread, Go Viral

It is a simple process to implement social sharing and bookmarking buttons into your blog articles.

If you want your content to spread, this is key.

This also helps your SEO.

4. Long-tail traffic and the importance of Great Content

Another part of SEO (and blogging) is considering keywords and phrases for the long term. The best way to explain this is to give you an example.

Our article, 3 Ways To Increase Your Chart Rank on ReverbNation, was written over a year ago but today remains the #1 read article on this site.

100% of the traffic comes from searches including phrases such as:

- how to raise rank on reverbnation
- how to cheat charts on reverbnation
- ranking reverbnation
- how to increase rank on...
- how to better band equity score
- how to increase reverbnation fans

And the list keeps going.

If you are clever with your website design, you can take the opportunity to direct this traffic to other parts of your website. But, again, this is easier said than done.

How does this apply to my band?

You create music in the blues rock genre but also receive a lot of influence from the classical guitarists you enjoy.

You are a studio geek and have a deep understanding of the gear and software used during recording.

Some ideas for creating blog content include:

- Buy albums from popular artists in your genre and write reviews on your band's blog – you have a chance at ranking high in searches for people trying to find reviews of Keb Mo's newest album.
- Blog a video of your band in the studio then write a paragraph or two describing the music, the songs, and the equipment or software you were using during the recording process. Including names of studios, engineers, or producers that worked with you can also help grab people's attention.
- If a piece of art, a book, a movie, a historical figure, or any other icon of mainstream culture influences one of your songs – blog about that song and explain how that book you just read inspired your newest lyric.

The possibilities are endless.

Notes

One of the best example's of a band implementing this strategy is <u>Mr. Hunter</u> of San Diego, California.

If you visit their website, their blog feeds into the front page so simply scroll down. Pay attention to the headlines and the content.

Their newest post is titled, <u>Mr. Hunter's Songwriting Secret Formula</u>, and discusses the creative process and the importance of setting a goal.

From this 1 article, the band has a chance of ranking in searches for "songwriting formula", "creative process", "songwriting goals", or other variations.

They have 14 pages of blog posts including songwriting strategies, photos of events, videos, pictures of their new equipment, and blogs about influences to their music.

Why and How ReverbNation Lost My Love

Summary: There was a time when I used ReverbNation daily to connect with fans, promote my music, and grow my network. Things were great. But then things started changing and I began using the platform less and less. I used to be an advocate for their services and now I find myself telling people not to bother.

Below I will share my perspective and experiences with the platform simply to provide insight to those who want it.

In the beginning...

Back in 1999, when I decided BUNKS was the musical direction I would take into the future; we chose to stay independent and use the Internet to promote and market the music.

There was no social media back then [as you currently experience it] but there were other ways to find and engage with the music community.

We were involved with various online communities through message boards and forums.

We engaged with hip hop heads on Rapmusic.com, Flowdoctors.com, Spitraw.com, and poetry forums such as Floetix. These communities were excellent places to make friends, share music, and collaborate with others. Unfortunately, Rapmusic is the only one that still exists.

Outside of Soundclick.com and Mp3.com (no longer exists). There was this other [developing] platform known as ReverbNation. I created BUNKS' profile and began using the service to connect with fans.

From a marketing standpoint, it is important to be where people are so this was another reason for choosing to use the platform.

Everything was great. People listened to our music, they took time to leave us messages, and other artists would communicate with us about collaborations and swapping gigs. When we put our first album on iTunes, we saw sales.

As the web evolved and ReverbNation grew, the company obviously had to evolve and change with it. A lot of RN's changes over the years have revolved around monetization and finding ways to charge musicians for premium services.

The price of not doing research

Many people accuse ReverbNation of preying on naïve artists. And I will have to agree with that [to a certain extent].

As much as we like to point fingers and blame others, it is YOUR responsibility (as an artist in chrage of your career) to educate yourself, seek guidance, and strategize before pouring money into anything...especially music promotion.

It's not ReverbNation's fault you pay them $250 for an advertising campaign that might do little to nothing for your music. You pay them, they provide the service....it's not really their problem if your ads suck or nobody clicks on them. Their job is to give you ad impressions on the major sites like MTV, Rolling Stone, and what have you.

It's also not their fault you are paying $17.95 a month for them to host your website when you could be using another service like Bluehost for $4.95/month.

Another thing that has always bothered me is the fact you have to spend $12.95/month for RN to host your RPK. That would be ok but you then have to pay anywhere from $5 to $20 just to submit that RPK to a gig, festival, or licensing opportunity.

You can see how quickly costs can start adding up.

If you are spending $250 to promote a show, will you make $250 at this show to cover that cost? If you are spending it to drive sales, how many sales do you have to make at .99 per song and 9.99 per album to recoup your expense? If you spend $250 submitting to gigs and other opportunities, will any of those opportunities move your career forward in a way that is worth that much?

> *There are plenty of bands who have the luxury of throwing money at the wall, but are you one of them?*

Let's say you pay $12.95/month for your RPK and then you spend around $50 to submit to 5 opportunities...that never respond to your submission. You just flushed that money down the drain.

Alternatively, I could use musicSUBMIT to create an EPK and then spend $99 to have that EPK submitted to 200 college radio stations that play urban music.

Would you rather have a chance at 5 opportunities or take your chances at earning new fans from 5 new radio stations? You are in control so you have the luxury of making this decision on your own.

There is no right or wrong answer, only what is right for the path you are walking.

With all of this said, (in a sense) they are taking advantage of naive artists - but they are not the only ones guilty of doing this online.

However, I am sure plenty of bands use ReverbNation's premium services and are doing just fine. Remember, this is my perspective based on my experiences.

Integration with Myspace

The moment my enjoyment of ReverbNation began declining is when they integrated with MySpace and allowed bands to blast emails to their MySpace friends (on top of their FanReach mailing list).

The moment this happened every band on MySpace and ReverbNation began spamming the hell out of each other. Why?

Because they know no better. Musicians are musicians...not marketers.

In 2008, I made money via digital downloads promoting through MySpace but when they integrated with ReverbNation it all came to a screeching halt. In fact, every thing I enjoyed about Myspace quickly went away. I have spoken with others who have shared this same experience so I know I am not alone.

Now, when I would log into MySpace, I would find 50+ messages in my inbox of nothing but ReverbNation FanReach blasts. This was a daily occurence.

It was aggravating, annoying, and a HUGE turn-off.

It suddenly became near impossible to effectively market music through Myspace because the fans were now pissed off by the RN band spam. Myspace was already dying but this put the nail in the coffin for me.

Also, more and more as time passed, it became clear that the only people signing up for RN FanReach mailing lists were other bands hoping you would subscribe back to return the "favor". Band spam does me no favors...neither do mailing lists with a 1% open rate.

This might have sparked the mass migration to Facebook (especially bands) but I have no data to back up this speculation. I remember a time when Facebook meant nothing to music marketing but obviously this changed with the launch of Pages.

I will say that ReverbNation's FB apps for band pages are/were pretty groovy but there are so many other options for Facebook this comment really has no weight.

The integration of Myspace with ReverbNation was the beginning of the end for me.

ReverbNation Promote It

ReverbNation is always changing, adding, and editing features but the next big thing that came after the Myspace fiasco was RN's advertising network - Promote It.

Now, if I had the money to spend AND knew I could get my return on investment (ROI), I would use this...but I am satisfied with Twitter Ads, Google Adwords, and Facebook Promoted Posts so I will stick with what works for us.

For $250 on up to $XXX, you can run advertising campaigns through ReverbNation that reach large networks such as MTV, Rolling Stone, CMT, VH1, Amazon, Datpiff, and many more.

Nearly every time I log into ReverbNation now, I am asked to start my free trial. But when I try to go through the steps to start my free trial, I get asked to pay so I have yet to try Promote It.

However, I do know that you can spend LESS money on other advertising networks and get MORE results.

For example, I can pay ReverbNation to promote a show on Facebook... but I could also just go to Facebook, set up an ad campaign for the show, and spend a lot less money to reach a larger, more precisely targeted audience over a longer period of time.

Since I cannot give you a proper analysis of Promote It, I will simply share my thoughts about it.

ReverbNation has a strong list of powerful networks which display their advertisements but unless you 1) have the budget, 2) have a solid strategy, and 3) know what you are doing or have guidance - it will turn into a waste.

If ReverbNation offers thorough help documents or any type of education program for PromoteIt, I am not aware. It would be nice if they did.

I say this because the average musician is not going to understand online advertising and marketing...much less how to plan, execute, and target an effective ad campaign.

You're not expected to know these things, you make music!

In my opinion, the price that RN charges to run these ads is not worth your dollars. Most DIY, indie musicians I know do not have the resources or funds to spend the type of money ReverbNation asks for their premium services and advertising.

Conclusion

Since we have been on the indie, DIY path for over 10 years...we are speaking to those of you just like us.

If you have a label, agency, or management behind you and can work with a decent budget, then your experiences are going to be a lot different on ReverbNation than mine have been.

What is the take away from all of this?

- THINK (critically) before acting blindly - especially when it comes to spending money to market your music. You can only be taken advantage of by your own ignorance.
- Do NOT pigeonhole yourself to one service or network. If ReverbNation works for you, then it works for you but if Facebook gives you better results...go spend more time on Facebook.

ReverbNation is a huge company that has been doing what they do for many years. I don't see them slowing down any time soon.

Why write this?

Once I got out of college and began working as an online music marketing consultant, it has been uber important for me to keep up with everything going on in the online sphere.

I am asked often "why facebook?", "should I use reverbnation?", "why do I need a website?", and other related inquiries.

After being asked the same questions over and over again, I decided to start blogging about marketing music on the web.

The most visited article (every day) on the Middle Tennessee Music blog is titled **3 Ways To Improve Your Rank on ReverbNation.**

The interesting thing is this article was published in 2011, but it is still one of the most viewed posts on the entire site. RN has even gone through 2 or 3 site re-designs since it was published.

100% of this traffic comes from search engines and people who are looking up info about ReverbNation. Below is a short list of the search phrases people use when they find this article.

- what do you do with reverbnation band equity
- how do i get higher ranked on reverbnation?
- how to get more reverbnation fans quickly without paying?
- where do you leave comments on reverbnation
- reverbnation charts important?
- how do charts work on reverbnation
- reverbnation chart ranking formula
- ...and many, many more

This means people all across the globe are working ReverbNation and trying to learn how to improve their band equity and chart ranks.

You can also see that people want to know how to use RN to grow without spending money. I see the search phrase "how to cheat reverbnation charts" pop up in our tracking data consistently.

This article is simply me sharing all of my thoughts, observations, and experiences in hopes to provide some insight.

Expert Interview on Social Media for Musicians with Joshua and Bret of Middle Tennessee Music

Interview conducted by Reputation.com.

Musicians are high-profile people that are watched by fans and critics alike, and scrutinized for their behaviors and comments. This media attention has only increased with the advancement of social networks.

Joshua Smotherman and C Bret Cambell, founders of Middle Tennessee Music, support independent musicians and help them get more recognition. They took the time to answer some questions about how musicians can benefit from social media and use it to their advantage while protecting their reputation.

Are musicians using social media in the best way to promote their careers? If not, what are some ways they can improve?

Joshua: It depends on which musician we are talking about, but in general, no. Everyone with an mp3 of a song they wrote is trying to fight for attention in a space and an industry they have never taken any time to study or understand. The average, DIY, indie musician is not educated in the fields of social media, marketing, PR, branding, or any of the other aspects of online promotion they need to understand, at least on the most basic level. The only way to improve is to ask for advice, do your own research, or watch your favorite band or artist and try to mimic the ways they use social media.

C Bret: We see many ways of using social media that are effective, and many that are not. The most common errors that we see involve "flooding" the streams of social media with the same post across multiple sites.

Others include:

1. Constant self-promotion
2. Talking only of one's self or own project
3. Not conversing, and only "broadcasting"

In general, the most egregious errors are made by independents that have no one to help. I would advise:

1. Following some of the "big names" and taking notes about their approach.
2. Finding a team of friends to post about you, so you don't have to.
3. Sharing the work with other actively engaging members of your community.
4. Responding to every message, mention, or question you can in a friendly manner.

This is just a start...

What is the best social media site for performers to build their brand?

Joshua: There is no "best", only what is right for you, the musician or band. The biggest mistake 99% of bands make is setting up profiles on every network possible and then sharing exactly the same updates across each one.

Unfortunately this is counter-productive. You need to narrow your use of social media to a select few channels. Use the ones where your fans and listeners are hanging out and, by trial and error, figure out what your fans on Twitter respond to and give them more of that; then figure out what Facebook responds to the best and give them more of that... each network is its own independent community and they need to be treated as such.

C Bret: The "best" is the one they are most comfortable with and which gets the best response. That said, Google Plus has become such a vibrant and innovative place, that I highly recommend every musician to set up a personal profile and a "band page." G+ offers many things that just can't be done elsewhere and the SEO benefits are amazing!

How should a musician respond to negative comments about their music, a performance, or something they did in the media?

C Bret: Simple. Thank the author for his or her input, and publicize the heck out of it.

Joshua: I agree with Bret. You are better off confronting it and using social media (and the comments section of the article, if it exists) to share your two cents and respond to these types of comments.

What is the best way for a musician to protect his or her reputation? How has the internet changed marketing for musicians?

C Bret: This begins with protecting your copyright by registering it. Beyond that, be nice, truthful and public. If you do those things, how can anyone speak ill of you?

The second part... well books have been written about it. Two years ago, the thought was something like, "Wow! Anyone can advertise and build a huge fan base for free! Let's jump on it!" At this point, the "social stream" is so flooded with musicians that we all must be very careful and professional, or we risk wasting all of our efforts to no avail.

Joshua: THINK before you act online. Everything you do is stored in a database somewhere for somebody to find. Most bands just jump online and start posting away with no strategy, guidance, or any type of plan for effective action. Social Media is a tool and it must be used wisely or you are only shooting yourself in the foot. Most bands are killing their image, their potential, and any chance of being noticed by those higher up in the music business by acting like idiots online.

You need a strategy and if you have no clue where to start, seek help from someone or start searching online for helpful articles related to online music marketing and the use of social media for effective results.

Are You Guilty? - 4 Ways Indie Musicians Are Killing Social Media

Originally published on CyberPR's blog.

In an ideal world I would wake up in the morning to a fresh cup of hot coffee. I would enjoy it as I check my e-mail and skim social networks to check up on friends and my favorite bands.

I would immerse myself in an online community of music lovers, songwriters, and musicians sharing, caring, and building with each other... NOT blasting commands to "check out my new hottest thing".

I see enough billboards on the interstate.

In this world:

- Bands would stop acting like rock stars and start acting like leaders
- They would build self-sustaining tribes
- They would listen to their fans
- They would understand that growing organically will always win over view counts

As a music blogger, my inbox would NOT be full of one-liners and YouTube links I only see as distractions. Whatever happened to "connecting" with someone?

Unfortunately, this world does not exist. From where I'm sitting, the average indie band sucks at using social media and its ruining it for everyone else. Most importantly, your potential fans.

What are we doing wrong, you say?

Oh boy...where do I begin?

Me, Me, Me Marketing

You might have been raised in a world of billboards and commercials, but using social media as a one way street is killing your promo game.

It seems too many people are missing the social half of the phrase, social media.

You need to engage with fans and listeners instead of blasting them with links, videos, and nonsense about buying your album.

Sadly, most bands qualify [as what the marketing world refers to] as spammers.

Engaging is easier than you think and should come naturally (assuming you are not a recluse).

- Share albums, videos, and news about other music you enjoy or local bands you play with.**Ask others what they think.**
- Share news related to the music industry or issues that reflect the personality of your band and use them to **engage in conversation.**
- Instead of posting links to the same videos and songs repeatedly, post clips of the band working in the studio or upload a demo mix and allow fans to share their opinions so you can take the art to another level. **Involve fans in your process(es).**
- **Network with bands** in other areas to create an atmosphere for gig swapping and collaboration as well as cross promotion of content.

This list goes on but the takeaway here is engage in a way that results in feedback and interaction.

Build a community.

Focusing on the wrong metrics

Your follower count means nothing unless you see conversions.

Huh?!

More important than a follower, view, or like:

- How many fans have signed up for your mailing list?
- Do you pass around a mailing list signup sheet at your show?
- How many people have you met at shows? (You do hang out with the audience after the show...right?)
- How many people have bought a CD or t-shirt?

Stop putting all your energy into increasing numbers on social sites and focus on converting the followers you have into loyal fans.

Use social media to funnel music listeners to your website where you attempt to convert them into a mailing list signup, song download, or merchandise sale.

Would you rather have 1,000 likes or 100 fans spending $1,000 on music, merch, show tickets and crowd funding campaigns?

Show me the money!

Repeating yourself on every social network

Sending your Twitter feed to Facebook then copying and pasting it to Google+ so the same message appears on every site is a horrible idea.

So is auto play on audio embeds but that's for a different time.

You are not expected to know marketing, you make music! Allow me to guide you on this train of thinking...

People who use Twitter are different than people who use Facebook and the people who use Google+ are not like the others.

It is imperative you consider these facts when developing a social media strategy and act accordingly.

Make sure you actually use social media as a music fan before deciding how to market your music using these tools. Follow bands who are in a position you would like to be in and see how they use each network. Notice what works, what doesn't work, and then perfect your plan of action.

Posting several updates to Twitter every hour (depending on the nature of the updates) is more acceptable than posting to Facebook every 15 minutes.

When you over saturate a person's FB News Feed, they hide you from their feed. Or worse...unlike your page or mark your posts as spam.

A general guideline is try to retweet, reply, comment, and share relevant content from others more than you broadcast and peddle your own wares.

Sell Without Selling

If you focus on building a community around your band instead of acting as a bulletin board, you will start noticing the true power of social media.

You will not see overnight results.

The key is to stay consistent, focus on creating great music, and communicate directly with your audience.

If you create a community of loyal fans, they will want to support you.

Your community will become your sales force and all you need to do is be yourself and continue giving fans a band worth loving.

Consistency allows you to reach a tipping point where fans begin promoting your music for you by wearing t-shirts, playing CDs at parties, and recommending you to their friends.

It is hard to conceive this when you are starting at zero, but 6 to 12 months down the road you will notice things happening simply because you remained persistent.

While fans are busy promoting your music, you need to seek out gig opportunities, blog reviews or interviews, and other chances to put yourself in the presence of tastemakers who can expose you to their audience.

Bloggers, journalists, booking agents, and other industry personnel will not give you their attention unless you have proof of a loyal, engaged following.

Buying followers or views might help you manipulate chart rankings and other metrics, but they will never replace the power of community. If you have 5,000 page likes but no one is liking, sharing, or commenting on your updates; we all see right through you.

So can the people who can expose you to bigger audiences of music fans.

In closing:

- Build your tribe
- Nurture your community
- Stop acting like a corporate sales machine

You might also be interested in this panel discussion concerning Marketing, PR, and Promotion on a Budget hosted by Indie Connect NYC which discusses mores things indie musicians are doing wrong online.

My Best Advice for Bands Using Social Media for Marketing in 2014

It's 2014 and the Internet is an infinite abyss of indie music, indie music blogs, pros blogging advice to musicians, musicians blogging themselves into nowhere, and a bunch of people pissed off they wasted so much money on ReverbNation and Facebook Ads last year.

And sadly, I've been hearing a lot more mediocre music than I feel I should be. Just because you have access to the interwebs does NOT mean you **make great music**.

Here's my best advice for DIY bands using social media for marketing in 2014...

1. **Make. Great. Music.**
2. Keep **Making Great Music** while you find a balance and a social media strategy that works FOR YOU, not against you.

Investing money into your music is now a must (in my opinion). Production, packaging, and marketing/PR are all things that separate the bands who are getting heard from the bands who are not. Doing some research and seeking professional help is definitely in your best interest if you plan on improving your music as a career.

I read an article earlier about how the music industry is dying and how that's good for us.

I am offering a couple of options for 2014...

Keep wasting all your time and/or money on social media while your art and live show suffers... OR

Spend more time creating the best music you possibly can and show us your full potential as a musician, songwriter, and artist.

- Stop thinking you are going to make a lot of money from music, specifically selling downloads. Invest in merchandise: CDs, t-shirts, stickers, buttons...
- Stop thinking the Internet will make you a rock star over night.
- Stop paying so much attention to social media and get out more. The relationships you develop offline are way more valuable than a few likes or RTs.

- Start building a tribe one supporter at a time.
- Start using the Web as a PR machine.

After **Making Great Music**, push it into the world and use music blogs and podcast features to **allow others to tell others** how **Great Your Music** is.

Being featured on 100 small blogs can push your awareness much further than anything I have seen bands doing on social media. Unless you have major label support, major funding, or the planets just happen to be aligned in your favor – **getting your music heard, appreciated, and shared by others is a lot of aggravating, depressing, never-ending, hard work.**

This year I encourage you to spend more time creating, more time performing, and more time engaging with the people who support you.

If you **Make Great Music**, people can and will find it.

This is one thing that the Internet has definitely accomplished for indie musicians — the ability to be found by anyone at any random time on this planet.

Links and Resources

Other topics we have published articles about:

- ReverbNation Tips and Strategies
- Website and WordPress Tips
- Make more of Google+
- More how to, info, and music business related articles

Bookmark our **resources** page for easy access to a list of tools, books, and services we recommend:
http://www.midtnmusic.com/resources/

Reviews:
http://www.midtnmusic.com/category/record-reviews/

Interviews:
http://www.midtnmusic.com/category/interviews/

Events: http://www.midtnmusic.com/event-coverage/

Podcast: http://www.midtnmusic.com/mid-tenn-listens/